Contents

Egypt boasts one of the oldest civilizations in the world, dating back more than 5,000 years. Modern Egypt is an exciting mix of traditional and modern cultures, of rich and poor, and of city and countryside. It is a major player in the politics and trade of both Africa and the Middle East.

IT STARTED HERE

Early civilization

Egyptian civilization contributed the first organized government to the world. Ancient Egyptians also developed methods of irrigation to help grow their crops, and they used the earliest known alphabet.

Where in the world?

Egypt is one of only three countries in the world (the others are Turkey and Russia) that lie on two continents. It is situated in north-east Africa and on the Sinai Peninsula, which is part of Asia. Although clearly an African country, the Middle Eastern influence is strong in Egypt. As well as its land borders, Egypt is bordered by the Mediterranean Sea in the north and by the Red Sea in the east.

An ancient civilization

One of the world's earliest civilizations grew up on the banks of the River Nile in Egypt. The river gave the ancient Egyptians water to grow their crops, and the surrounding desert provided protection against attack from other peoples. For 3,000 years, Egyptian culture – based on a religious belief in the afterlife – flourished.

▼ *Egypt has land borders with the Gaza Strip and Israel to the north-east, Sudan to the south and Libya to the west.*

COUNTRIES IN OUR WORLD

YPT

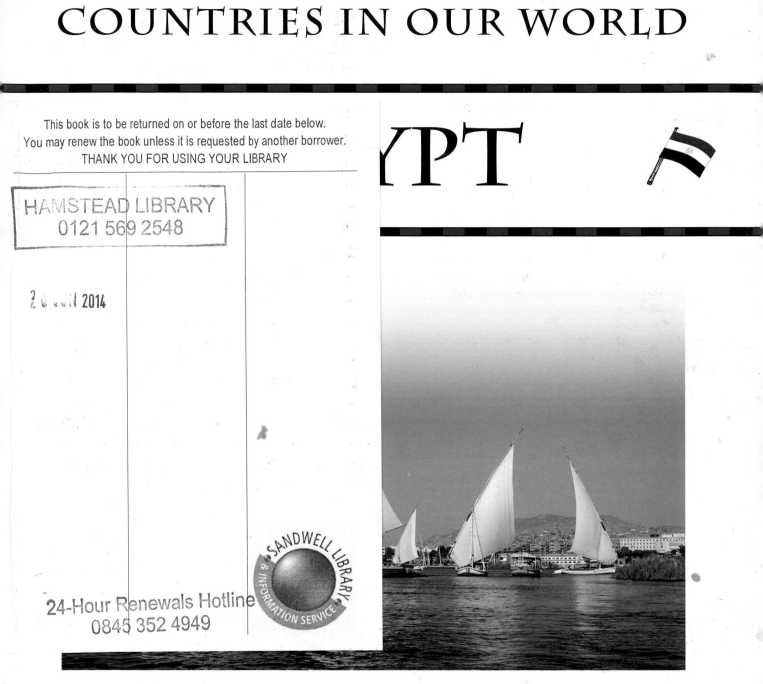

Ali Brownlie Bojang

W
FRANKLIN WATTS

This edition 2012

First published in 2010 by
Franklin Watts
338 Euston Road
London NW1 3BH

Franklin Watts Australia
Level 17/207 Kent Street
Sydney NSW 2000

Copyright © Franklin Watts 2010, 2012

Produced for Franklin Watts by
White-Thomson Publishing Ltd
+44 (0) 845 362 8240
www.wtpub.co.uk

Series consultant: Rob Bowden
Editor: Sonya Newland
Designer: Clare Nicholas
Picture researcher: Amy Sparks

A CIP catalogue record for this book is available
from the British Library.

Dewey Classification: 962'.05

ISBN 978 1 4451 0808 7

Printed in Malaysia

Franklin Watts is a division of Hachette Children's
Books, an Hachette UK company

www.hachette.co.uk

The Egyptians built huge pyramids, sphinxes and statues as tombs and monuments to their rulers, called pharaohs.

Influences and occupations

From 341 BCE, Egypt was ruled by a series of invaders from Persia (now Iran), Greece and Rome. In the seventh century, the Arabs came to Egypt and introduced the Islamic religion and the Arabic language. The Arabs ruled Egypt for the next 600 years, until the Turks conquered them in 1517 and took control of Egypt.

IT'S A FACT!

The Great Pyramid of Giza is the only one of the Seven Wonders of the Ancient World that is still standing. It is 147 m (482 ft) tall, and was the tallest monument in the world until the nineteenth century.

▼ *In the desert outside Cairo stand remains of the ancient Egyptian civilization – the Sphinx and the Great Pyramid of Giza.*

Britain and Egypt

During the nineteenth century, both France and Britain took an interest in Egypt, and helped to pay for the building of the Suez Canal in 1869. This created a 163-km (100-mile) 'short-cut' from Europe to India and the rest of Asia. Ships no longer had to go all the way around Africa. This was very important to countries like Britain that were trying to increase their influence over world trade. In 1882, Britain seized control of the Egyptian government to safeguard its interest in the Suez Canal. For the next 70 years Britain had some control over Egypt, although there was still an Egyptian king and an Egyptian prime minister and parliament.

GOING GLOBAL

The Suez Canal is an important trade route. In 2010, 17,993 ships passed through the canal. Between 2000 and 2008, the amount of shipping from Southeast Asia and the Far East which passed through the canal increased by two-and-a-half times, showing how important the canal has become for Chinese exports to Europe.

▼ *Around 8 per cent of all world trade passes through the Suez Canal on container ships. The Suez Canal Authority is working to make the canal deeper, so that supertankers can travel along it.*

The Egyptian republic

In 1952, a group of soldiers led by Gamal Abdel Nasser staged a revolution. They intended to overthrow the king, Farouk, who they thought was corrupt and too influenced by the British. The revolution was a success and the monarchy was abolished. In 1953, the new Egyptian republic was born.

▲ *Gamal Abdel Nasser (waving), leader of the revolution and second president of Egypt, drives through the streets of Cairo.*

Egypt's place in the world

Egypt is still a major channel for international trade. The country's role as a go-between and mediator in the Middle East is also becoming more important. Egypt has a good relationship with the USA and the European Union (EU). Despite internal unrest in 2011, which led to President Mubarak stepping down, Egypt continues to be a key player in the Arab world.

BASIC DATA
Official name: **Arab Republic of Egypt**
Capital: **Cairo**
Size: **1,001,450 sq km (386,662 sq miles)**
Population: **82,079,636 (July 2011)**
Currency: **Egyptian pound**

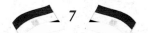

Egypt is a plateau made up of sand and rock. Across this dry landscape flows the longest river in the world, the Nile, and on either side of the river are fertile valleys. The Nile is the lifeline of Egypt, providing water for drinking and crops.

The River Nile

The Nile flows for 1,545 km (960 miles) through Egypt, creating a green line through the desert. In the past the river would flood every year and leave behind a fine fertile silt. This created an area up to 12 km (7.5 miles) either side of the river where farming could take place. With the help of irrigation, people were able to grow a wide variety of crops, such as cotton, rice, corn, wheat, beans, fruit and vegetables. They also kept cattle, water buffalo, sheep and goats. Today, the flooding of the Nile is controlled by the Aswan High Dam.

IT'S A FACT!

The Nile Delta, where the river spreads out and flows into the Mediterranean Sea, is one of the largest deltas in the world. It covers 240 km (150 miles) of the Mediterranean coastline and is about 160 km (100 miles) from north to south. The Nile Delta is the winter home of some of the largest groups of birds in the world, including little gulls and whiskered terns.

▼ *Traditional Egyptian boats, called* feluccas, *sailing on the Nile.*

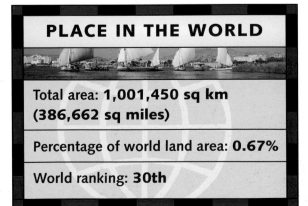

Climate

There is very little rainfall in Egypt and everywhere is hot and dry. The capital, Cairo, receives no more than around 10 mm (0.4 in) of rain a year, which usually falls in the cool season between December and February. Further south the amount of rainfall decreases even more, and in some desert locations it may rain only once every few years. During April, dust storms are common, caused by the hot Sirocco wind that blows from the Sahara Desert.

▲ *Tourists protect their faces from the sand and dust in Cairo.*

PLACE IN THE WORLD

Total area: **1,001,450 sq km (386,662 sq miles)**

Percentage of world land area: **0.67%**

World ranking: **30th**

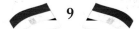

The deserts

About 95 per cent of Egypt is desert. In this harsh environment, where temperatures can reach over 50°C (122°F), very few plants, animals or people can survive. To the west lies the Western Desert, which is actually part of the Sahara Desert – the largest desert in the world. This is a relatively flat area, covering about two-thirds of the country, where strong

▲ *In Egypt's deserts, the wind creates limestone rock formations and high sand dunes.*

winds have blown the sand into dunes more than 30 m (100 ft) high – as tall as a 10-storey building. Here, the wind also forms large limestone outcrops. To the east of the country lie the more rocky and mountainous Eastern and Sinai deserts.

Highs and lows

The highest point in Egypt is Mount Catherine, which lies towards the southern tip of the Sinai Peninsula and is 2,629 m (8,625 ft) high. Mountainous peaks running down the coast of the Red Sea reach 750 m (2,461 ft). In the Western Desert there are vast low-lying hollows. The largest of these is the Qattara Depression, a huge area of saltpans and rocks. At 133 m (436 ft) below sea level, this is the second-lowest point in Africa.

Environmental problems

Egypt's exceptionally dry climate and its large population create huge demands for water and fertile land. Vital farmland is being taken over by the growing cities and, in some places, lost to the deserts. To produce more food from less land, farmers use more fertilizers and pesticides on their crops. These pollute the River Nile, adding to the pollution from sewage and waste from the cities. The Red Sea, with its coral reefs, is also threatened by oil pollution and increasing tourism.

IT'S A FACT!

Global warming is causing sea levels to rise, threatening Egypt's low-lying but densely populated delta area and the ability to grow crops there, as well as destroying many of its ancient structures. Scientists predict that by 2020, more than 15 per cent of the valuable delta area will have been lost, and use this as a warning to other countries about what may happen if climate-change issues are not addressed.

▼ *This area of the Nile Delta could be flooded in a few decades as a result of global warming.*

Egypt's population of just over 82 million is the largest of any Arab-speaking country, and the third largest in Africa after Nigeria and Ethiopia. Most of the people live on the small strip of land around the River Nile. Egypt's population has grown rapidly in recent decades.

Who are the Egyptians?

Egypt's inhabitants are a mix of races, descended from the ancient Egyptians, Berbers from other parts of North Africa and sub-Saharan Africans such as the Nubians. There are also groups descended from the Arabs, Greeks and Turks. Most Egyptians live along the fertile banks of the River Nile and in its delta. There are small communities of people in the oases of the Western Desert and in the oil-drilling and mining towns of the Arabian Desert.

PLACE IN THE WORLD

Population: **82,079,636**

Percentage of world total: **1.16%**

World ranking: **15th**

▼ *Nubia covers part of southern Egypt and stretches into northern Sudan. Here, a Nubian woman collects water from a canal running through her village near Aswan.*

City living

Over 40 per cent of the population lives in cities such as Cairo, Alexandria, Subra al-Haymah and Luxor. Egypt's cities have grown quickly. In 1850 the population of Cairo was 250,000; today it is around 11 million and it is the largest city in Africa. The populations of the cities swell daily as people commute to work from the towns and villages nearby.

Population density

About 95 per cent of Egyptians live along the Nile, on about three per cent of the land area. This concentration has created one of the most densely populated areas in the world. On average there are 1,540 people per sq km, while the density in the whole of Egypt is 77 people per sq km. In comparison, the population density of the UK is 246 and for Africa as a whole it is 65 people per sq km.

IT'S A FACT!

In the deserts of Egypt live small groups of Bedouins. Although they are divided into different tribes, they have several similar customs and are known for their folk music and dance. In the past, Bedouins were nomadic – they moved around throughout the year – but today many of them live in permanent settlements in desert areas, and some have also now settled in Egypt's large cities.

▼ *Alexandria is the second largest city in Egypt, with a population of more than 4 million.*

Population growth

Egypt's population has grown very rapidly in recent years. It more than doubled between 1970 and 2000. Although the rate at which it is growing has slowed down now, it is still increasing by about 1.5 million people every year. One-third of Egyptians are under 14 years old, and in the near future they will be looking for work, houses and healthcare, as well as schools for their own children.

Pastures new

Job opportunities in Egypt are scarce and salaries are low. Many Egyptians leave the country to find work and higher wages in Saudi Arabia and other countries in the Middle East, Libya, the USA or Europe. In 2009, it was estimated that 6.5 million Egyptians were working in other countries. Some of these people are well-qualified, working in jobs such as engineering and teaching.

▼ *Although life expectancy at birth is quite high (72.66 years), Egypt has an extremely young population. Only 4.5 per cent of the population are over 65.*

Desperate to leave

Others have little education and few skills, and in their desperation to improve their lives they cross the Mediterranean Sea to Europe on makeshift boats. It is a dangerous journey, and some die on the way when their boats sink. Some travel to Egypt from other countries especially to take this boat journey, if they are unable to leave from their own countries. Illegal immigration like this has risen over the past 10 years, but it is impossible to know how many people have successfully reached and settled in Europe. Some experts think it may be as many as 20,000 people a year.

GOING GLOBAL

The money that Egyptians living abroad send home is very important to their families and to Egypt as a whole. In 2010, Egyptians sent home almost US$8 billion, which has helped the Egyptian economy.

▼ *Illegal immigrants from Egypt and other countries in North Africa arrive in Italy.*

Culture and lifestyles

Egyptian culture is a mix of the old and the new. It has absorbed ideas and traditions from its invaders and visitors over thousands of years, and combined these with its own ancient traditions.

Religion

The Arabs introduced Islam to Egypt in the seventh century, and today times of business meetings, films and concerts are decided by the sound of the call to prayer from the minarets five times a day. Ninety per cent of Egyptians are Muslim. In recent years some Egyptians have started to support a stricter form of Islam, and more and more women are covering their heads and faces with a veil, or *hijab*. Most other people – around nine per cent – are Coptic (Egyptian) Christians, making up the largest Christian population in the Middle East.

▶ *A mosque in the city of Hurghada on the Red Sea coast. This mosque is quite modern – built around 30 years ago – but Islam has been the main religion here since the seventh century.*

IT STARTED HERE

Writing

It is thought that the first true alphabetic writing started in Egypt in around 2000 BCE, based on an even older system of hieroglyphs – small pictures used to represent words. Experts think that most alphabets in the world today are based on the ancient Egyptian system of writing.

Family and food

Family is important to all Egyptians, although today Egyptian families are getting smaller, as people are choosing to have fewer children. Food is an important part of the hospitality shown to visitors in Egypt. Typical dishes are made from beans and lentils, rice and flatbreads, and vegetables cooked in onions and tomatoes. Egyptian food is similar to that in neighbouring countries such as Greece, Lebanon and Turkey. In the cities, however, wealthy Egyptians frequently eat European food. French cuisine and Western fast food are particularly popular.

IT'S A FACT!

All Egyptian children must attend school between the ages of six and 14. Education is free in government-run schools, although there are private schools available for the children of wealthier Egyptians. Arabic is the official language in Egypt, but many schools also teach French and English.

▼ *Western-style fast food is popular in Egypt's large cities. This sign for McDonald's is written in Arabic, Egypt's official language.*

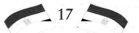

GOING GLOBAL

Many ancient Egyptian objects, such as statues of pharaohs and mummies, can be found in museums all over the world. Some of the best examples are in the British Museum in London, the New York Metropolitan Museum of Art and the Louvre in Paris. Touring exhibitions, such as those showing the treasures of the pharaoh Tutankhamun, have been sell-outs in countries such as the UK and USA.

▲ *This obelisk, known as Cleopatra's Needle, once guarded an ancient temple at Luxor. Now it stands in Paris's Place de la Concorde.*

Life in the countryside

Country life in Egypt is very different from life in the cities. In the Nile Delta, for example, there are still peasant farmers, called *fellahins*, wearing the traditional baggy trousers. Most people in rural areas are very poor.

Life in the cities

In contrast, life in the cities is similar to that in cities all over Europe and the USA. Busy urban areas such as Cairo and Alexandria are packed with people. There are traffic jams, blaring horns, office buildings, shopping malls and restaurants. Despite these signs of Western life, however, only a few of Egypt's city dwellers are as wealthy as Europeans or Americans, and standards of living in Egyptian cities are lower than in these countries.

Music

Traditional music in Egypt has been influenced by Arabic music from Persia and India, and its tones and rhythms are very different from Western music. This music is usually played at weddings and other festivals, but young Egyptians prefer pop music, and there are many modern pop singers in Egypt today. Many of these base their music on the traditional forms. Two of the most popular singers are Mohamed Mounir and Amr Diab.

THE HOME OF...

Arabic films

Egypt has been nicknamed the 'Hollywood of the Arab world', and is the major supplier of films in this region, producing around 40 a year. An international film festival is held every year in Cairo, and this has gained renown not just among Arab countries, but also those in the Western world.

Sport

Football is the most popular sport in Egypt, both for playing and watching. Egyptian football clubs, especially El Ahly and El Zamalek, are known throughout the Middle East and Africa. The national team is popularly known as The Pharaohs, and it is the most successful African football team, having won the African Nations Cup six times. Other popular sports in Egypt are basketball, handball, squash and tennis. Egyptian runners are also admired all over the world for their speed and stamina.

▼ *Egypt's national football team celebrates winning the African Nations Cup in 2008 after the final against Cameroon.*

Economy and trade

Only three per cent of Egypt's land can be used to grow crops, but 32 per cent of the population is involved in farming. The activities that bring in the most foreign money to Egypt are the production and export of oil, tourism, money sent home from Egyptians working abroad and fees from shipping companies using the Suez Canal.

Natural resources

Oil is Egypt's most valuable natural resource, and in the 1990s Egypt also began exporting natural gas. Both of these are mined near the Red Sea, on the Sinai Peninsula and in the Western Desert. Phosphate rock (used to make fertilizer), iron ore and salt are also mined in Egypt. Egypt is self-sufficient in energy, which means it does not rely on other countries for its energy needs. As well as oil, Egypt generates hydroelectricity using the enormous Aswan High Dam. The dam is used to control the Nile floods. However, it also stops some of the silt from being carried down the river, which means the soil in some areas is not as fertile as it used to be.

▼ *The Aswan High Dam provides around 20 per cent of Egypt's electricity, but it has caused concern because of the effect it has had on the quality of soil downriver.*

Farming

Nearly all farms in Egypt are located in the Nile Valley and Delta. Traditional farms are small and are irrigated with water from the Nile. On larger, more commercial farms, the land is worked more intensively and fertilizers are used to get the most crops possible. There are usually two crops a year and the main cash crop – crops grown especially for export rather than for personal use – is cotton. Some desert land is being developed for farming, but these schemes are very expensive. Water has to be either transported by pipes from the Nile, or very deep holes have to be dug to reach underground water supplies.

GLOBAL LEADER

Egyptian cotton

Egyptian cotton is considered to be the best in the world. It is used to produce high-quality sheets for top department stores, and clothes for many well-known high-street shops. However, it is estimated that about a million children in Egypt are employed to help with the cotton harvest, often working in very bad conditions.

Trade

Egypt buys more from other countries than it sells to them, which is one reason why Egypt is in debt. Egypt exports its oil and ready-made clothes, cotton and other farming products such as citrus fruit and rice. It sells these mainly to the USA and Italy. It buys machinery and transport equipment, food, chemicals and wood products mainly from the USA, China, Germany, Italy and Saudi Arabia.

▶ *Workers in a t-shirt factory. Clothes are big business in Egypt because of the high-quality cotton that can be grown there.*

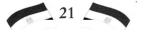

Industry

Egypt has some manufacturing industries in cities such as Cairo and Alexandria. These produce mainly iron and steel, textiles, plastics and cars. There are also several oil refineries. Some international companies, such as car manufacturers, have been attracted to Egypt because it has such a large population, which not only provides buyers for the manufactured goods, but also workers who can be paid low wages compared to what the companies would pay for labour in their own countries.

Small businesses

Small businesses can be found in many of Egypt's city streets. Here, people may repair household items or cars, recycle metal, litter or fabrics, or sell all different products either in small shops or on market stalls. Many of these businesses are not registered and people do not pay their taxes. It is impossible to know how many people work in this informal way, but the number has been estimated at 7 million.

GLOBAL LEADER

Mubarak Pumping Station
The Mubarak Pumping Station is the largest in the world. It pumps water from Lake Nasser to the Toshka Depression, a large low-lying area of desert. The pump facility is 30 m (100 ft) wide, 140 m (460 ft) long and 60 m (197 ft) high. It was built in a pit around 15 storeys deep, and is 10 times the size of a football stadium.

▼ *In the markets of Egypt, vendors sell locally made handicrafts such as textiles and objects crafted from metal.*

▲ *The clear, warm water and the variety of fish and coral reefs of the Red Sea offer some of the best scuba diving in the world.*

Tourism

With its good weather, fascinating history, monuments such as the pyramids and the temples, and its beautiful Red Sea resorts such as Sharm-el-Sheikh and Dahab, Egypt is one of the world's top tourist destinations. In 2010, almost 15 million tourists visited Egypt but the following year numbers dropped dramatically due to political uncertainty caused by the revolution. The largest numbers of tourists usually come from Italy, followed by visitors from Germany, the UK and France. Tourism has been affected by the bad state of the global economy in recent years and will hopefully pick up again once the global economy and Egypt's government are more stable.

THE HOME OF...

Scuba diving

The year-round high temperatures, low rainfall, warm seas and beautiful coral reefs have enabled the Red Sea town of Sharm el-Sheikh to develop from a small fishing village into one of the world's top scuba-diving resorts.

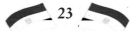

23

Government and politics

Egypt is a republic, which means it is not ruled by a monarch, but by representatives elected by the people. Since 1953 it has had a president and a prime minister who shared power.

Ruling Egypt

Although the president and the prime minister shared the responsibility of ruling Egypt up until spring 2011, the president had some powerful roles. He supervised the drawing up of the country's laws and was also head of the armed forces. When the street protests in January and February 2011 led to the resignation of President Mubarak, who had been president since 1981, a military council took over in order to usher the country towards democracy.

▼ *Protestors filled Tahrir Square in central Cairo in February 2011, demanding that President Mubarak step down as president.*

The first president

In 1953, when Egypt became independent, the leader of the revolution, Gamal Abdel Nasser, became its president. He wanted to unite all the Arab nations under Egyptian control, so he turned to the USSR for help. This angered the countries of the West.

Al-Sadat and Mubarak

The next president, Anwar al-Sadat, distanced Egypt from the USSR and tried to make peace with Israel. This angered some Egyptians and he was assassinated in 1981. After almost 30 years, Hosni Mubarak stepped down as president on 11 February 2011. He worked hard to build Egypt's strength but kept the country under emergency law, an almost military regime that curbed basic freedoms. In 2011 he was put on trial for corruption charges and for his part in the death of hundreds of protestors.

FAMOUS EGYPTIAN

Anwar al-Sadat (1918–81)

In 1978, President Anwar al-Sadat received the Nobel Peace Prize for his role in improving relations between Egypt and Israel, which he shared with the Israeli prime minister, Menachem Begin. However, in 1981 he was killed by assassins from secret groups who wanted to make Egypt a pure Islamic society and who felt he had betrayed Egypt and Islam.

▼ *Anwar al-Sadat (left), shortly before he was assassinated. Hosni Mubarak is on the right.*

Egypt and Israel

For many years Egypt and Israel were sworn enemies, and between 1948 and 1978, the two countries fought three wars. However, in 1978, US president Jimmy Carter brought together the warring sides. As a result, a peace treaty was signed between Egypt and Israel, making Egypt the first Arabic-speaking country to recognize Israel as a nation. Since then peace has prevailed between the two countries but the relationship has become tense and more distant in recent years.

Human rights

Several international human rights organizations, such as Amnesty International and Human Rights Watch, have criticized Egypt's record on human rights. Women do not have the same rights as men, and more and more women are calling for equal rights. During President Mubarak's time, people who disagreed with him were tortured and put in jail. Since the revolution in spring 2011, there has been continued concern about human rights abuses.

▼ *Egyptian journalist Yomna Mokhtar used the social networking site Facebook to campaign for rights for unmarried women, who are regarded as inferior in Egypt.*

International links

Egypt is a member of several influential international organizations, including the Arab League, the African Union and the United Nations. Membership of these groups allows Egypt to have a say about many international issues, and to play a significant role in world events, such as trade agreements and peacekeeping missions in troubled countries.

▼ *Boutros Boutros-Ghali (left) on a visit to Rwanda during his time as Secretary-General of the United Nations.*

FAMOUS EGYPTIAN

Boutros Boutros-Ghali (b. 1922)

Boutros Boutros-Ghali was born in Cairo in 1922. He was an Egyptian diplomat and became the sixth Secretary-General of the United Nations, holding this position from January 1992 to January 1997. During his time as Secretary-General he had to deal with issues such as the Rwandan genocide, the Angolan Civil War and the wars in the former Yugoslavia.

One of the biggest challenges Egypt faces is the need for land and water to provide for its growing population. This issue could be made more difficult by the threat of climate change.

The need for land

As the overcrowded cities of Egypt continue to expand, they will take up valuable farming land. To solve this problem, the government has started some major projects to develop the deserts. By 2017, it estimates that it will have converted 1.5 million hectares (3.5 million acres) of dry, sandy desert into productive farmland. Water for these projects is provided by deep wells that tap into a huge water reserve beneath the Sahara Desert.

▲ *As Egypt's population continues to grow, slums are springing up on the outskirts of the cities. Providing adequate housing is a priority for the Egyptian government.*

The need for water

As Egypt's population grows there will be a greater need for water for homes, for crops, for factories and to create power. One big concern is what countries up-river on the Nile do to affect the waters. As they take more

water to fulfil their own needs, for example, it may decrease the amount of water available to the Egyptians. Although there is an agreement in place about water use, some experts think tension over water could lead to the world's first 'water war'.

Climate change

Climate change, and the rise in sea levels, is a major threat to the food-producing Nile Delta region. Scientists have predicted that the Mediterranean will rise between 30 cm (12 in) and 1 m (3 ft) by the end of the twenty-first century. This would flood coastal areas along the Delta.

Developing a modern country

For thousands of years Egypt has faced the limitations of its deserts and climate. It will continue to face these – and other – challenges. Many Egyptians want to see great political changes, including the transition to democratic government. Egypt will continue to be an important player on the world stage, too.

▼ *Dealing with the dry climate is one of Egypt's biggest challenges, but ancient treasures such as the pyramids and great temples will continue to attract tourists and boost the economy.*

Glossary

Arab someone who belongs to a race of people that originated in the Arabian Peninsula.

cash crops crops that are grown especially to be exported to other countries.

Christianity a religion that follows the teachings of Jesus Christ.

coral reefs underwater structures formed from the remains of sea creatures.

economy the financial system of a country or region, including how much money is made from the production and sale of goods and services.

export to transport products or materials abroad for sale or trade.

feluccas traditional Egyptian sailing boats with flat bottoms and triangular sails.

global warming the gradual rise in temperatures on the surface of the Earth, caused by changes in the amount of greenhouse gases in the atmosphere.

gross domestic product (GDP) the total amount of money a country earns every year.

immigrant a person who has moved to another country to live.

irrigation supplying dry land with water by means of ditches and channels.

Islam a religion with belief in one god (Allah) and his last prophet, Muhammad.

Muslim a follower of the Islamic religion.

nomadic moving from place to place, often to find the best grazing land for herds of livestock.

oasis a fertile or green area in a desert where there is a source of water.

plateau a raised area of land, usually fairly flat and sometimes also called 'tableland'.

pollution spoiling the environment with man-made waste such as vehicle emissions, waste gases from factories, or chemicals from fertilizers.

population density the number of people living in a square kilometre or square mile of a country.

pyramids large structures built as tombs for the ancient Egyptian pharaohs.

republic a form of government in which a country is ruled not by a king or queen, but by officials elected by the people.

rural relating to the countryside.

saltpans small, undrained, shallow depressions where water builds up and evaporates, leaving salt behind.

silt fine particles of earth deposited by rivers.

Further information

Books

River Adventures – Nile
by Paul Manning
(Franklin Watts 2012)

Egypt (Cultures of the World)
by Patricia Levy and S. Levy
(Marshall Cavendish, 2007)

by Nicole Frank and
Susan L. Wilson
(Franklin Watts, 2006)

*The Changing face
of Egypt*
by Ron Ragsdale
(Wayland, 2007)

Settlements of the River Nile
by Rob Bowden
(Heinemann, 2006)
Welcome to Egypt

We're from Egypt
by Victoria Parker
(Heinemann Library, 2005)

Websites

http://www.touregypt.net/Kids/
A site for children offering a virtual tour of Egypt, with information about its history and monuments as well as games and activities.

www.bbc.co.uk/news/world-africa-13313370
A detailed and up-to-date site from the BBC.

http://www.travelforkids.com/Funtodo/Egypt/egypt.htm
Take a journey through Egypt with this fun site, from Cairo to the Valley of the Kings.

http://www.socialstudiesforkids.com/subjects/economics.htm
Get to grips with economics on this site where topics such as money, trade and budgets are explained.

Every effort has been made by the publisher to ensure that these websites contain no inappropriate or offensive material. However, because of the nature of the Internet, it is impossible to guarantee that the content of these sites will not be altered. We strongly advise that Internet access is supervised by a responsible adult.

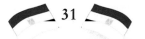

Index

Numbers in **bold** indicate pictures